New Approaches
to Fieldwork

Geographical
Association

Theory INTO Practice

PROFESSIONAL DEVELOPMENT
FOR GEOGRAPHY TEACHERS
Series editors: Mary Biddulph and Graham Butt

New Approaches to Fieldwork

DAVID CATON

Geographical
Association

Acknowledgements

I would like to thank Steve Rogers, David Job and Paul Weedon for their support and encouragement. Thanks are also due to Gaye Mapp for her guidance on the uses of literacy in the field.

The author

David Caton is Head of Geography at Shrewsbury Sixth Form College.

The series editors

Mary Biddulph is Lecturer in Geography Education in the School of Education, University of Nottingham, and Dr Graham Butt is Senior Lecturer in Geographical Education in the School of Education, University of Birmingham.

1005309346

ISBN 1 84377 169 1
First published 2006
Impression number 10 9 8 7 6 5 4 3 2 1
Year 2008 2007 2006

Published by the Geographical Association, 160 Solly Street, Sheffield S1 4BF.
Website: www.geography.org.uk
E-mail: ga@geography.org.uk
The Geographical Association is a registered charity: no 313129.
The Publications Officer of the GA would be happy to hear from other potential authors who have ideas for geography books. You may contact the Officer via the GA at the address above. The views expressed in this publication are those of the author and do not necessarily represent those of the Geographical Association.
Editing: Lester Betts
Design and typesetting: Ledgard Jepson Ltd
Printing and binding: In China through Colorcraft Ltd, Hong Kong

Contents

Editors' preface

Theory into Practice is dedicated to improving both teaching and learning in geography. The over-riding element in the series is direct communication with the classroom practitioner about current research in geographical education and how this relates to classroom practice. Geography teachers from across the professional spectrum will be able to access research findings on particular issues which they can then relate to their own particular context.

How to use this series

This series has a number of other concerns. First, we seek to achieve the further professional development of geography teachers and their departments. Second, each book is intended to support teachers' thinking about key aspects of teaching and learning in geography and encourages them to reconsider these in the light of research findings. Third, we hope to reinvigorate the debate about how to teach geography and to give teachers the support and encouragement to revisit essential questions, such as:

- Why am I teaching this topic?
- Why am I teaching it in this way?
- Is there a more enjoyable/challenging/interesting/successful way to teach this?
- What are the students learning?
- How are they learning?
- Why are they learning?

This list is by no means exhaustive and there are many other key questions which geography teachers can and should ask. However, the ideas discussed and issues raised in this series provide a framework for thinking about practice. Fourth, each book should offer teachers of geography a vehicle within which they can improve the quality of teaching and learning in their subject; and an opportunity to arm themselves with the new understandings about geography and geographical education. With this information teachers can challenge current assumptions about the nature of the subject in schools. The intended outcome is to support geography teachers in becoming part of the teaching and learning debate. Finally, the series aims to make classroom practitioners feel better informed about their own practice through consideration of, and reflection upon, the research into what they do best – teach geography.

Mary Biddulph and Graham Butt
Spring 2006

Introduction

Fieldwork provides many geography teachers and students with some of their most significant and enjoyable educational experiences. Most geographers will be able to recall times spent in the field that have had particular value for their educational, professional or even personal development. The quality of that experience will reflect the place and topic being studied and the people involved in the teaching and learning. It is also very likely to be influenced by the type of activity that takes place. This can vary from a scientific, quantitative approach to qualitative, affective activities such as poetry and drama. It is these different methods of fieldwork that are the focus of this book.

For some years now, fieldwork in secondary schools has been dominated by three main genres: the teacher-led field excursion, a hypothesis-testing model known as 'field research' and an enquiry-based approach. Each has its own approach to teaching and learning, so the choice over how fieldwork is done has a very real influence over the outcomes. But how often do we stop to reflect on why we use a particular approach to fieldwork? The purpose of chapter 1 is to inform this discussion by examining the purposes, strengths and weaknesses of these three approaches to fieldwork.

This kind of reflection on ways of working in the field has led an increasing number of geographers to suggest that there is an area of understanding that is often overlooked or undervalued. While traditional approaches offer many things, there is also a case being made for fieldwork activities that set out to actively engage students with the place they are visiting and provide them with a more rounded, holistic appreciation of that environment. A wide variety of fieldwork activities using a qualitative methodology have been developed to achieve these aims. While labels such as 'sensory' or 'discovery' have been given to fieldwork within this genre, the term 'experiential fieldwork' used by Rowles (1978) is perhaps most useful, as it implies both a spirit of discovery and an engagement with the environment. The main purpose of this book is to introduce this approach and examine what it has to offer both teachers and students.

The nature of experiential fieldwork is introduced in chapter 2 and its origins and purposes are discussed in more detail in chapter 3. The following two chapters introduce in more detail some ways of using experiential activities to tie in with current concerns in secondary school geography. The model outlined in chapter 4 is an extended writing activity supported by experiential fieldwork, thinking skills and formative assessment while chapter 5 explores some qualitative and quantitative uses for descriptive words in the field.

The underlying purposes of this book are twofold. Firstly, it is hoped that it will encourage deeper reflection and informed discussion on how fieldwork is done in secondary schools. The second purpose is to present a range of qualitative, experiential techniques that can be used in secondary school fieldwork.

Photo: © John Halocha

1: Mainstream approaches to teaching in the field

A useful starting point when deciding on what methods to use on a field exercise is to ask ourselves what outcomes we are hoping to achieve from the visit. Job, Day and Smyth (1999) have identified the following five purposes for fieldwork:

- **Conceptual:** developing knowledge and understanding
- **Skills:** developing organisation and technique
- **Aesthetic:** developing sensitivity to and appreciation of landscapes, places and environments
- **Values:** developing awareness of a range of viewpoints
- **Social and personal:** developing self-confidence and teamwork

Since each approach to fieldwork gives different priority to these purposes, the decision over which style of fieldwork to use will greatly affect the type of outcomes that result. In this chapter the purposes and merits of each of the mainstream approaches to fieldwork will be considered in order to help teachers make informed choices about which approach to take.

The field excursion

The aim of this approach is to 'read' the landscape by recording its human and physical components and the links between them (see, for example Wooldridge and East, 1951). The teacher's role is that of an expert guide, providing information in a didactic manner. Students might take part in activities such as field sketching, description or answering questions. The focus is on developing conceptual knowledge, but skills such as writing, sketching and map reading may be developed as well. A further outcome is that students may develop some level of aesthetic appreciation of the environment (Job, Day and Smyth, 1999).

Although not frequently used as the sole method on a trip, teachers may draw upon aspects of this approach when their main purpose is to develop their students' knowledge and understanding. It has the convenience of allowing the teacher a good deal of control over learning. However, the students' role is often fairly passive, which can have implications for levels of concentration and motivation. Most geography teachers will appreciate the difficulty of holding the interest of large groups of students when using this method outdoors, particularly when the area is noisy and distracting. There can also be a tendency towards description, causing this type of fieldwork to lack intellectual rigour. Furthermore, the activities undertaken on a field excursion do not lend themselves to explaining or testing the relationships between the different components in the landscape (Job, 1999). In practice, however, the incorporation of question and answer sessions can go a long way towards addressing this limitation.

Field research

This type of fieldwork emerged in the late 1960s as part of the growth of quantitative techniques in geography as a whole and has become the most commonly used method in secondary schools (Rhynne, 1998; Job, Day and Smyth, 1999). A reductionist approach is used, in which a specific theme in a small area is studied using a detailed, scientific-style method, and students structure their investigation to test hypotheses (now more commonly softened to become questions and sub-questions) (see Figure 1). The approach derives from a technocentric world-view, in which the earth is viewed as a machine that can be understood, predicted and managed through the use of scientific research and the application of ingenuity and technology (Job, 1996).

A number of geographers have considered the limitations of this approach, with criticisms directed at the lack of intellectual stimulation that is created. McPartland and Harvey (1987) argue that the sequence that is followed to test a hypothesis tends to follow a fairly predictable course, with few surprising elements to stimulate interest. Furthermore, once the students have mastered the recording techniques, the fieldwork activities themselves can descend into a repetitive collection of data.

Further criticisms have been made at the level of conceptual learning achieved through quantitative fieldwork. A significant reason for this is that greater emphasis is often placed upon the development of techniques than on developing knowledge and understanding (Rhynne, 1998). Research by Harvey (1991) highlights how explanation of patterns and processes usually takes place in front of a set of results in the classroom, rather than in the field where the subject matter can be experienced first-hand. His research also found that the transfer of conceptual learning from quantitative fieldwork to examinations was poor, largely because students were not effective at linking their results to a wider geographical context. Conceptual learning can also be constrained by having a rather narrow focus on a few links within a system, such as the factors that affect patterns of land use in a city centre or plant species on a sand dune. Furthermore, a reductionist approach discourages students from seeing some of the more complex interrelationships in geography, particularly between physical and human factors and between local and global scales (Harvey, 1991; Job, 1996).

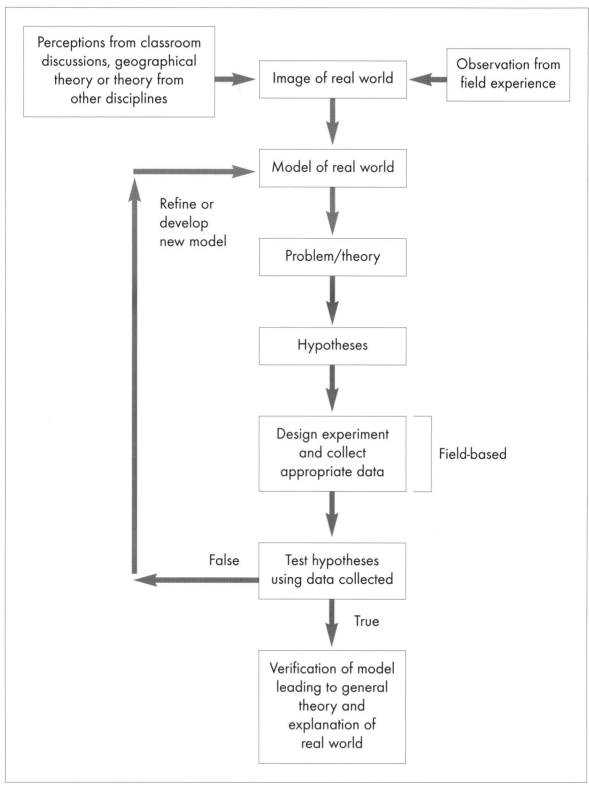

Figure 1: A framework for field research. After: Job, 1999.

Questions have also been raised about the type of learning outcomes that tend to result from field research. Job (1996) suggests that when drawing conclusions from fieldwork using this approach there is little opportunity for values to be considered, such as the implications of social inequalities in urban areas or the impact of a flood defence scheme on people's quality of life. He also argues that studies using field research will often lead to rather simplistic conclusions that reflect, rather than challenge, society's prevailing acceptance of technological engineering solutions to problems. Furthermore, by restricting fieldwork to only factors that can be measured, consideration of non-quantifiable aspects of places such as sounds, smells, beauty and atmosphere is neglected. As a consequence, there is little recognition of what makes a place unique, reducing the subject to '... the study of *any* stream or *any* town' (Pocock, 1983, p. 319).

These qualities that make places different and interesting have the potential to stimulate students' feelings and reactions, especially when visiting for the first time. Many geography teachers will recall how students respond to places such as a dramatic viewpoint, rundown coastal town or vibrant city centre by forming questions and opinions. A number of authors have suggested that field research is not well suited to taking advantage of the positive environment that interesting places can create (see, for example Brough, 1983; Harvey, 1991; Job, 1999; Van Matre, 1979). This can be attributed to the fieldwork being focused on one specific theme as well as the lack of an affective dimension to learning (Kent and Foskett, 2002).

So why has field research achieved this position of dominance in secondary school fieldwork? Rhynne (1998) cites the influence of the GCSE and A level examination boards, which tend to assume the use of this method and thus inhibit alternative approaches. She also points out that, under pressure to make the best use of limited time in the field, teachers are using this approach as a way to quickly cover skills and concepts in readiness for examinations. A further factor is the natural tendency for teachers to draw on their own experience, which preserves the status quo. Of course, this way of doing fieldwork does have significant merits. Teachers and students alike find it reassuring to follow a clear structure that often neatly leads to simple conclusions. Also, the method can sometimes offer the satisfaction of disproving hypotheses based on traditional models, such as that river velocity increases with distance downstream (Job, 1996). Useful vocational skills are developed, both in the field and also when processing, presenting and analysing results. Some practitioners feel that using a quasi-scientific approach adds status to the fieldwork (Job, 1996). Finally, both students and teachers often enjoy the active, sometimes fairly physical, collection of data.

Enquiry-based fieldwork

This approach emerged during the late 1970s in an attempt to get students more actively involved in fieldwork and increase the practical relevance of physical geography in the field. The focus is on issues rather than hypotheses, due to the concerns that were increasingly being voiced at the time about human mismanagement of resources and the environment (Job, 1996). The methods used to investigate the geographical question or issue are usually quantitative, but qualitative activities might also be used to find out about people's opinions.

Enquiry can be effective at developing conceptual understanding as it involves evaluating results, relating conclusions to their wider geographical context and making links between different areas of the subject. Skills of interpretation, evaluation and decision-making are developed, to add to those of data collection and handling. A further benefit of enquiry is that it requires students to pay attention to the characteristics of the place being studied. However, this does not usually extend as far as developing a personal response to its aesthetic qualities. A final strength of enquiry is that, by getting students to deal with conflicts relating to live issues and form their own opinions, this approach can generate high levels of interest and motivation (Job, 1999).

While the enquiry approach addresses some of the limitations of field research, there remain questions over the depth of understanding and engagement with places that it creates. Job (1996, 1999) points out that enquiries often focus on the location of a development, such as a by-pass or superstore, with students stopping short of questioning whether development should take place and what form it should take. He also argues that students are usually presented with the issues on which enquiries are based, and suggests that participation and opinion-forming would be enhanced by developing investigations from the students' own experience. Nevertheless, the most successful enquiries can go some way towards addressing these issues and the method is well suited to studies that involve choices and opinions. However this approach, in common with field research, is not geared towards developing affective understanding or promoting a deep interest in, or concern for, places and nature.

Photo: © Helen Sail

Photo: © Helen Sail

2: The experiential approach to teaching in the field

Although fieldwork in secondary schools is dominated by the three approaches discussed in the previous chapter, alternative methods based on qualitative information are becoming more widely used. There is quite a varied collection of activities within this genre, but they can perhaps be encompassed by the term 'experiential fieldwork' since they have the common theme of promoting meaningful experience with the environment. The aim of this chapter is to introduce this approach to fieldwork.

It would perhaps be helpful to start with a case study which looks at how different types of fieldwork might be used to investigate issues in rural settlements. A glance at some fieldwork textbooks provides us with a collection of quantitative techniques that could be used within either the field research or enquiry framework. These might include surveys of housing age, type and quality, house prices, services and environmental quality as well as using census data and questionnaires (Holmes and Farbrother, 2000; Frew, 1993; Lenon and Cleves, 1994). These activities will provide a range of quantitative data about various aspects of a village, which in turn offers opportunities for data handling, presentation and analysis.

The following case study shows how the same rural settlements might be investigated using experiential fieldwork.

Case study

The students begin by looking at cards containing ideas and questions that provoke reflection and observation, such as 'Imagine how this village might have been different 100 years ago' and 'What are the main colours in this landscape?' (see Job, 1999). When using these cards, the students are encouraged to investigate parts of the village that arouse their curiosity and to focus on the questions that interest them most. Local people are then approached to draw maps of the village from memory. The conversations that develop while they draw provide information about the village that is anecdotal, personal and engaging. Looking at the resulting maps reveals the features that are important to the residents and that give the place its character. Students then work in small groups to act out scenes from the life of the village, taking on roles and reacting to real and potential changes such as the closing of the village post office or the opening of a caravan park. Old and new buildings are compared using descriptive words, poems and sketches. The students then sit in silence to record any sound that they hear, noting the direction it comes from, what makes the sound and whether it enhances or detracts from the quality of the environment. To finish, the students try to sum up their perceptions of the village by choosing one feature or event that they feel epitomises the place.

The approach to learning in this case study is one of a spirit of discovery, described by Rowles (1978) as a 'gentle inquisitive concern with the environment' (p. 174). The students are given as much freedom as possible to explore the aspects of a place that interest them and to develop their own response to the environment. Ward and Fyson (1973) argue that environmental education becomes far more meaningful to students when it relates to the way in which they perceive and respond to their surroundings. In this way, learning can be guided by the observations and questions of the students, giving them greater ownership over their work. The teacher acts as a facilitator, creating the conditions under which students can find out for themselves. Hall (1981) suggests that the students' minds should be 'neither filled nor moulded by the teacher' (p. 3): if a teacher dominates this type of fieldwork it might inhibit learning. For example, if students are given too much factual information they may be less willing to discover things for themselves and if they are given opinions they may find it less easy to develop their own.

This student-centred outlook encourages a holistic approach in which all aspects of an environment are embraced, rather like the way in which holistic medicine treats the whole person. In contrast to the fairly confined outcomes of the quantitative activities, investigation is opened up to include those aspects of a place that might not fall into traditional definitions of geographical subject matter or that cannot be easily measured. Speake and Fox (2000) provide an effective example of this by showing how studying street art and popular culture can enhance our understanding of city centres. As well as enabling students to investigate the things that awaken their curiosity, this holistic approach provides a more rounded understanding of places. By way of example, Figure 2 illustrates how using experiential fieldwork in rural settlements can lead students to consider features such as colours, sounds and architecture that provide a place with its unique character.

A fundamental purpose to this style of fieldwork is to engage students with the place that they are visiting so that they have a meaningful experience of that environment. This is described by Seamon (1979) as a 'heightened contact' with a place, in which participants become more aware of themselves and the world around them. Tuan (1974) describes how people's bond with their environment is aesthetic, tactile and through their feelings. Experiential fieldwork activities encourage greater awareness of these aspects of places by getting students to observe, describe, reflect and use their senses. Students are also encouraged to examine and express their feelings about the place they are studying in order to develop understanding on an affective or emotional level.

Fieldwork activity	Outcomes
Discovery cards	• Observation, discussion and reflection on a wide variety of aspects of the environment, including change, sustainability, safety, environmental quality and pollution
Mental maps	• Learning what gives a place its character • Learning what features of a place are important to different people • Experiencing village society through conversations with local residents
Drama	• Understanding the impact of change • Identifying with different opinions and attitudes
Descriptive words and poems	• Observation and evaluation of old and new built environments • Making aesthetic judgments • Developing personal opinions
Sketching	• Observation and evaluation of old and new built environments
Sound map	• Recording of how sounds contribute to environmental quality • Making aesthetic judgments
Choosing an epitome	• Reflection on what makes a place unique • Reflection on personal perceptions of a place

Figure 2: Outcomes from experiential fieldwork in rural settlements.

The use of a qualitative methodology provides students with the flexibility and subtlety needed to develop personal, affective and aesthetic responses to the environment and to develop understanding of non-quantifiable qualities such as sounds and feelings. In many examples of experiential fieldwork these have been adopted from the humanities and social sciences. Daniels (1992) illustrates how the sensibilities and approaches used in art and literature (to which drama could be added) are effective in developing a sense of place. They encourage students to look closely, reflect and examine their own feelings. The importance of the senses in creating the unique character of an environment has led to the development of sensory fieldwork methods. These employ ways of getting students either to look more closely or to use hearing, smell and touch in order to develop awareness, empathy and understanding (Pocock, 1983; Daniels, 1992; Job, 1999). A further group of activities use various forms of dialogue as a way to develop understanding and opinions (Cosgrove and Daniels, 1989).

Photo: © Andrew Williams

3: The thinking behind experiential fieldwork

This chapter will look more deeply into the thinking that has led to the development of experiential fieldwork and examine what it can offer to teachers and students.

The affective dimension

Research has shown that engaging the feelings and emotions of students in the field can be beneficial for the development of conceptual understanding (Foskett and Kent, 2002). It has also been found that when fieldwork consists of memorable experiences and the senses are engaged, students are better able to remember what they have learned (MacKenzie and White, 1982). Slater (1994) goes further by questioning the way in which objective, intellectual knowledge is often separated from subjective feelings in geography lessons (an accusation that could be levelled at a good deal of fieldwork) (see also Reid, 1986). She argues that students should be encouraged to explore their feelings and develop their own personal responses alongside their objective learning. This will allow them to touch upon subjective aspects of places, such as the moral and aesthetic dimensions, that might otherwise be neglected. Using this holistic approach encourages students to appreciate the richness and complexity of places, providing them with a context that can help to link ideas in their minds. She also argues that by combining thinking and feeling, students are better able to appreciate the values that underlie people's attitudes, giving greater depth to understanding of their opinions. As we have seen, questions have been raised over the levels of conceptual understanding and recall of information that are achieved when fieldwork is viewed as a quantitative, scientific activity. Perhaps approaching fieldwork from the perspective of the social sciences or humanities might add greater depth and breadth to students' understanding, providing them with a more rounded educational experience.

Sense of place

The purpose of a number of experiential activities is to develop a sense of place. Relph (1976) describes how this is created by a combination of three things. The first of these, the physical features of an environment, are the focus of experiential activities that encourage close observation and description (some of these are described in chapter 4).

Students might also be encouraged to look deeper at the underlying significance of physical features, such as how the amount and type of security measures can reveal levels of fear of crime (Ley, 1992). A second aspect of sense of place is illustrated by Goodey (1982):

> 'The urban context is largely a human one and our feelings about places reflect more the glances or gazes of other people's eyes, snatches of conversation, clothes and appendages, than the built-form environment' (p. 21).

The ways that people contribute to the character of a place might be investigated through observing, recording and reflecting on the activities that take place in a human environment such as a village or city centre. The idea of sense of place also involves the feelings that people have about places and the meaning that places have for them. An example might be how an inner urban neighbourhood may be valued by some of its residents for its close and vibrant community, while others living in the same place may feel socially isolated and vulnerable.

Attempts to revive the importance of a sense of place have come as a response to the growth of placelessness in modern society. This involves both a decline in the distinctiveness of different places and a weakening of the bond between people and their local environment (described by Tuan (1974) as 'topophilia') (Relph, 1976). Goodey (1982) and Huckle (1981) identify various influences in modern society, such as mass culture, media stereotyping and by-passing travel, that have eroded people's ability to sense place. They also attach some blame for this to geographical education. The discipline, with its ideographic (place-seeking) tradition, is well suited to addressing the problem of placelessness. However, the scientific approach, with its focus on space, location and generalities, often provides only a superficial knowledge of places (Daniels, 1992). By taking students to the places that they are studying, fieldwork is the most natural context for developing a sense of place. This opportunity may however be missed if fieldwork does not adequately address the students' interests and questions about their surroundings (Harvey, 1991). Job (1999) goes further to argue that '... by not valuing and nurturing a sense of place through our experiences in the field, we have unwittingly contributed to a growing and creeping sense of placelessness' (p. 1).

Participation

Many experiential activities have been developed with the purpose of promoting positive social and environmental change. Fien (1992) describes this learning with a more radical purpose as education 'for', rather than 'through' or 'about' the environment. An important figure in this aspect of experiential fieldwork has been Steve Van Matre, whose Sunship Earth programme attempted to promote care and respect for nature through activities that encourage a deeper experience of the environment (Van Matre, 1979). Randall (1999) shares this ecocentric purpose, describing how experiential methods can encourage students to be confident and creative about the future society that they would like to be a part of, and empowered to help bring it about. Brough (1983) argues for the importance of developing aesthetic appreciation in the field to help create a society whose members can effectively judge what we make and do in order to 'overcome the greyness and lack of feeling that threaten us' (p. 63). The model used by Job (1999) and Hawkins (1987) shows how experiential activities might encourage students to care enough about the places that they are studying to want to become actively involved in the issues that arise from their fieldwork, perhaps through writing letters or taking part in community projects (see Figure 3). Palmer and Neal (1994) illustrate this approach by describing a project in which students took an active role in shaping the future of some sewerage disposal ponds. Initial fieldwork, including observation of birds as well as using their sense of smell, persuaded the students that the ponds were worth protecting: a goal that they helped to achieve through collecting information and raising public awareness.

Some examples of experiential fieldwork take education for the environment a stage further by involving students in practical activities for social and environmental change. Job (2002) describes how a study of woodland ecology might develop beyond its conclusion stage to involve students in coppicing and working with the wood to make craft products and furniture. At the Centre for Alternative Technology in Wales students learn about sustainability through involvement in practical activities such as composting (Randall, 1999). This approach challenges the students to consider the values that they hold by demonstrating alternative ways of living. Anticipating the concerns that teachers might have about the practical difficulties of organising this type of activity, Job, Day and Smyth (1999) point out the possibilities created by schemes such as the Ecoschools programme and Agenda 21 for enabling students to become actively involved in the issues arising out of their fieldwork.

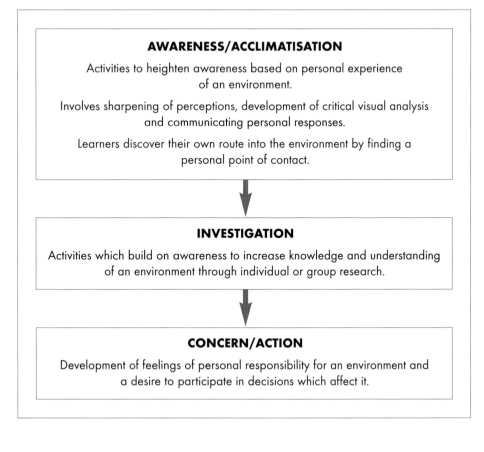

Figure 3:
A framework for using fieldwork to encourage concern and action.
After: Hawkins, 1987; Job, 1999.

AWARENESS/ACCLIMATISATION

Activities to heighten awareness based on personal experience of an environment.

Involves sharpening of perceptions, development of critical visual analysis and communicating personal responses.

Learners discover their own route into the environment by finding a personal point of contact.

INVESTIGATION

Activities which build on awareness to increase knowledge and understanding of an environment through individual or group research.

CONCERN/ACTION

Development of feelings of personal responsibility for an environment and a desire to participate in decisions which affect it.

Photo: © Helen Sail

4: Using experiential fieldwork to support extended writing

In the activity introduced in this chapter, extended writing provides a focus for working in the field and develops literacy skills and conceptual learning on return to the classroom. The role of fieldwork in this activity is to develop awareness of the place of study, to help students to form their own opinions and to encourage them to empathise with the views of others. This activity would be appropriate in any location in which significant change has taken place, such as a commuter village, inner city or tourist honeypot.

Preparation for the visit

Wittrock (1974) argues that learning in the field is more effective when based upon prior knowledge. For this activity, students will benefit from preparatory work to develop their understanding of the main issues in the study area. This will provide them with a basis of understanding with which to interpret the environment. The students are also given a writing objective on which the follow-up work will be based. For the example used here, the writing task is based on the premise that a former resident of a small rural town has asked the local school to send letters describing how the place has changed since she moved away 20 years ago (Figure 4).

In the field, stage 1: acclimatisation activities

The fieldwork begins with some acclimatisation activities. These are intended to increase the students' awareness of their surroundings and encourage them to develop a personal, affective response to the environment through use of the senses, close observation and reflection. It is hoped that they might develop an interest in some aspects of the place that they are studying and start to form questions and opinions. The issues that might be raised can be developed in the second part of the fieldwork and subsequent follow-up activity. These activities also anticipate the theme of the writing task by introducing the students to aspects of the place that might have changed.

How is Bridgnorth changing?

> 20, Pond Road,
> Washington
> USA
> 20th May
>
> Dear Mrs Chapman,
>
> You won't remember me, but I am a former pupil of your school. I lived in Bridgnorth for the first forty years of my life and was very fond of the town. Twenty years ago this week I moved with my family to live in America to start a new job. Now I have retired I often think about Bridgnorth and wonder how the town has changed since I left.
>
> I was wondering if some of your students might be interested in writing to me to tell me how Bridgnorth has changed in the past 20 years. I am very interested in what changes have taken place, why they have happened, and how different people feel about these changes. Perhaps they could do some research to find these things out.
>
> Many thanks in anticipation,
>
> Margaret Wilson

Write a letter to Mrs Wilson about some of the changes that have happened since she left Bridgnorth 20 years ago.

For each change that you mention you should include:
- A description of the change
- Some explanation of why the change has happened
- Thoughts about how different people feel about the change

Figure 4: Using a writing task to provide structure and purpose to fieldwork.

1. Sketching

The choice of what to sketch and how will reflect an individual's own interpretation of a scene (Pocock, 1983). Relph (1976) suggests that one small feature can capture the essence of a place. By asking students to sketch the single feature that epitomises their view of a place, they are encouraged to reflect upon what gives an environment its identity as well as their own perceptions (Smith, 1993). This activity has the advantage over photography that it encourages students to look closely and subjectively at their surroundings (Pocock, 1983). It provides time for reflection and discussion, which can help students to develop a sense of place. It also calls for close observation of the aspects of a place that create its character, such as shapes, textures, colours and materials.

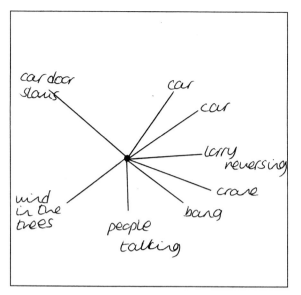
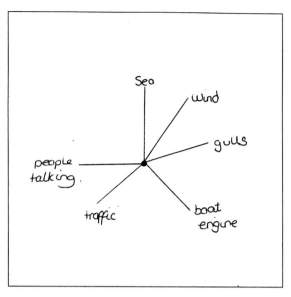

Figure 5: Sound maps produced by students in the field.

2. Observing activities

Listing the things that people are doing, however mundane, gives further opportunity for observation and reflection, as well as providing an insight into the nature of local society. An alternative approach would be for students to imagine that they are a video camera fixed at a vantage point and to describe what it sees as it watches the street (George, 1997).

3. Sound maps

This involves drawing a line from a point on a page in the direction of any sounds that can be heard (examples are provided in Figure 5). By doing this in silence and possibly blindfolded or with their eyes closed participants are forced to listen and concentrate. Focusing their attention upon using this one sense helps students to listen more carefully and to become more discriminating about sounds (Schafer, 1977).

4. Questioning

The questions in Figure 6 use thinking skills, particularly those of fluency and originality, to develop awareness and understanding of a place. These could be issued on cards, which can be shuffled and the top question answered (see Job, 1996).

Figure 6: Questions to encourage thinking skills in the field (developed from George, 1997).

What would happen if there were no cars allowed here?

How could you improve this place?

Think of new names for roads/buildings/squares and explain why you have chosen them

List all the good things about this place. Which are the most valuable?

How many reasons can you think of for living here?

Think of headlines to describe what might have happened here.

A plenary discussion can be used at this stage in order to direct the outcomes from these activities towards the writing task. Listing as many changes as possible that might have happened in the past 20 years requires students to return to the notes made during the acclimatisation activities and also to look again at their surroundings. Providing period photographs of the same location could help to stimulate ideas.

In the field, stage 2: completing the planning frame

The planning frame (Figure 7) provides a structure for recording ideas from the acclimatisation activities in preparation for their use in the extended writing task. It guides students from description towards higher order thinking, thus reflecting the assessment criteria in the National Curriculum attainment target and GCSE and A level specifications.

To complete the planning frame students, working either alone or in a group, choose one feature that has changed, such as the construction of new houses or a supermarket. They describe this feature in detail in the first box of the planning frame. The teacher's role might be to encourage students to observe closely and choose interesting adjectives.

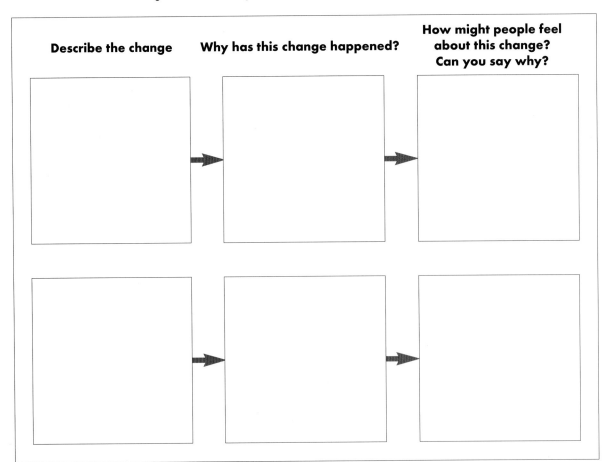

Figure 7: Planning frame: How has this place changed in the past 20 years?

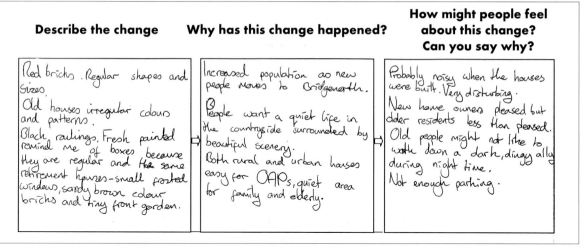

Describe the change	Why has this change happened?	How might people feel about this change? Can you say why?
Red bricks. Regular shapes and sizes. Old houses irregular colours and patterns. Black railings. Fresh painted remind me of boxes because they are regular and the same retirement houses – small frosted windows, sandy brown colour bricks and tiny front garden.	Increased population as new people moves to Bridgenorth. People want a quiet life in the countryside surrounded by beautiful scenery. Both rural and urban houses easy for OAPs, quiet area for family and elderly.	Probably noisy when the houses were built. Very disturbing. New home owners pleased but older residents less than pleased. Old people might not like to walk down a dark, dingy ally during night time. Not enough parking.

Figure 8: *Notes made by a year 7 student in the field using the planning frame.*

The possible reasons for this change are then discussed and entered in the next box along, drawing on knowledge gained in the preceding lessons. In the final box in the row, thoughts on how local people might feel about this change are recorded (see Figure 8). Further rows are available for notes to be made in the same way about other changes that have been noticed. The planning frame can be adapted to include different stimulus questions to suit the place of study, subject content and the age and ability of the students. Further support can be provided for less able students by using a scaffolding approach (illustrated in Figure 9).

Throughout the activity, questioning and discussion can be used to enhance the quality of responses. For example, fluency can be encouraged by asking for a range of alternative reasons for change, or empathy, by asking how a five-year-old or 70-year-old might feel about an issue. Allowing the discussion to respond to the interests and opinions of the students gives them greater ownership of their work. An illustration of this is provided by the reaction of my own students to traffic drowning out their conversation as it came uncomfortably near to their position on a narrow pavement. This experience stimulated discussion about how the town might be different if traffic were banned from the High Street. It might also be possible to engage more able students in a running exchange of questions about the issues that arise from observing and discussing a scene. Using Socratic dialogue in this way can help students to examine not only their own opinions, but also the assumptions on which they base those ideas (Cosgrove and Daniels, 1989).

Follow-up to the fieldwork in the classroom

Maintaining a sense of place after returning from a trip relies upon reviving memories of the visit. This can be encouraged with an opening activity in which students are invited to recall sounds, shapes, smells and textures. The main activity is to produce a piece of polished extended writing in response to the writing task presented prior to the field visit. Brownsword (1998) shows how extended writing encourages students to justify their

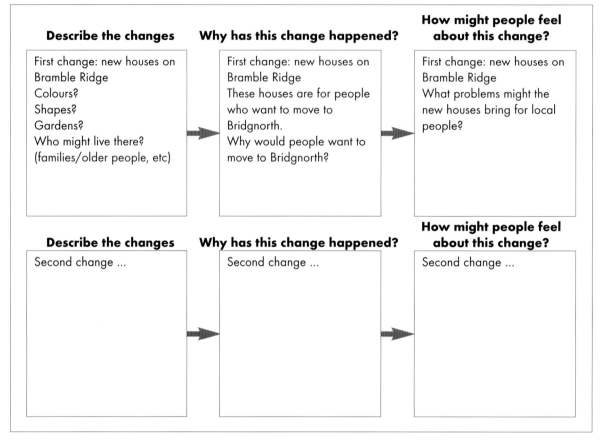

Figure 9: *Planning frame using a scaffolding approach.*

ideas, so that teachers can learn about the depth of their understanding. The writing process also involves working with ideas and making links, which helps to develop geographical understanding. Since extended writing is an effective vehicle for expressing values, reflections and feelings, it is a natural form to convey the outcomes of experiential fieldwork.

Differentiation

In extended writing activities, less able students often need help to organise their work and understand what is expected of them (Counsell, 1997). In this example it is provided through formative assessment and modelling.

Formative assessment

Assessment criteria have an important role in raising attainment by improving students' understanding of quality in their written work (George et al., 2002). This understanding can be enhanced by involving students in assessment activities, such as proof reading, evaluating or redrafting work, either alone or with a partner. Introducing these criteria prior to the activity can help to show students what makes a good piece of work for someone at their level. Formal assessment of extended writing also provides clear information about an individual's performance. This enables effective feedback to be given as to how a student can move up to the next level (Black and Wiliam, 1998). Figure 10 shows some simple assessment criteria for the case study used throughout this chapter. These have been developed using a strand of the National Curriculum attainment target but could equally be adapted from examination board assessment criteria. An alternative would be to base assessment levels upon literacy criteria, in order to focus the students' attention on developing their writing skills. This would give greater prominence to literacy learning objectives, which can help to improve the quality of writing in geography (Butt, 2001).

Level	Reasons for change	Viewpoints about change
2	Describe Bridgnorth	Give your views about change in Bridgnorth
3	Simply describe changes in Bridgnorth	Give reasons for your views about change in Bridgnorth
4	Describe changes in Bridgnorth	Give simple reasons for different people's views about change in Bridgnorth
5	Give simple reasons for changes in Bridgnorth	Explain reasons for different people's views about change in Bridgnorth
6	Give more detailed reasons for changes in Bridgnorth. Show links between processes of change	Explain why people have different attitudes to change in Bridgnorth

Figure 10: Levels adapted from the National Curriculum attainment target (used for assessing the writing task shown in Figure 4).

NC Level	Level descriptor
4	Explaining that one feature is caused by another (e.g. new houses have been built due to people moving to the village).
5	Explain **how** one feature is caused by another **or** explain that one feature causes another which causes another (e.g. people moving into the village has created a demand for houses, resulting in more being built).
6	Explain **how** one feature causes another, and then **how** that happens (e.g. the pleasant rural environment has encouraged people to move to the village. This has caused demand for housing, resulting in more being built).
7	Explain how two causes **work together** to create one feature that causes another (e.g. people wishing to move away from the pollution and congestion of the city are attracted to this pleasant rural environment. This has caused demand for housing, resulting in more being built).

Figure 11:
Assessment grid focusing on the quality and depth of explanation in a writing task.
After: George et al., 2002.

George *et al.* (2002) offer an alternative set of criteria for formative assessment that identifies levels of sophistication in the explanation offered by students. Using this approach, levels 4 to 7 of the attainment target could be replaced by the criteria shown in Figure 11. The assessment criteria could even be extended to allow credit for understanding difficult concepts or for the quality of description.

Modelling

The example shown in Figure 12 illustrates a model paragraph structure. The theme of the paragraph is introduced in a topic sentence, then developed through description, explanation and finally, opinions. In this way, the information follows the sequence of each row of the planning frame used in the field. The model also demonstrates how to meet the three main literacy objectives chosen for this example:

- Structure your paragraphs carefully
- Get a balance between describing and explaining
- Use punctuation correctly.

Dear Ms. Wilson,

I am writing to reply to your question about how Bridgnorth has changed in the past twenty years.

Since you left Bridgnorth a bypass has been built on the southern edge of the town. This road crosses the river over a concrete bridge. It was built because traffic had become very congested in the town centre. Visitors to Shropshire are pleased with the road, as it makes their journey quicker. However, the people living close to the bypass have to put up with noise and pollution from the road. This may have caused the value of their houses to fall.

Figure 12: A model letter to illustrate assessment criteria.

Figure 13 shows how challenging targets for more able students can be introduced and illustrated using the same process.

Be clear about your **audience**
- Be formal – you have never met her
- Be personal

Choose your **vocabulary** carefully
- Adverbs (such as *usually, normally, quite*) can make your meaning clearer
- Use interesting adjectives that describe accurately

Use an **interesting style**
- Start sentences in different ways, such as with a verb or adjective
- Use complex sentences – words like *then, when, which* and *who, because, though* make good linking words

---

Dear Ms. Wilson,

I am writing to reply to your question about how Bridgnorth has changed in the past twenty years.

Since you left Bridgnorth a bypass has been built. It crosses a bridge that stretches across the river at the southern end of the town. It was built because traffic had become quite congested in the town's narrow streets. As you can imagine, visitors to Shropshire are pleased with the road because it makes their journey quicker. However, residents have to put up with the constant droning of traffic as well as air pollution from the road. Some local people feel that the bypass has caused the value of their houses to fall.

Figure 13: A model letter to illustrate more challenging targets for literacy.

To involve the students more in the modelling process, a topic sentence can be provided and students asked to offer their own version of how the paragraph could develop. In order to make vocabulary more interesting and precise, students could offer alternative words to some of those provided in the model. They could be challenged to use alliteration or to suggest fresh, unusual vocabulary that evokes a feeling or makes the reader think. This activity could be supported by use of a thesaurus and individual whiteboards on which alternative words could be displayed for discussion. Finally, discussion could focus on alternative ways of starting sentences (illustrated in Figure 14).

Figure 14: Some alternative ways of starting sentences.

Sentence structure	Example
Subject–verb–object	'The building stands shabby at the corner.'
Beginning with the adjective	'Shabby, the building stands on the corner.'
Using a prepositional phrase	'Standing in/walking through the churchyard ...'

Photo: © Margaret Mackintosh.

5: Using descriptive words in the field

Relph (1976) describes how people's choice of words to describe aspects of places, which might include adjectives such as 'ugly', 'useful', 'alienating' or 'enjoyable' (p. 47), reveals something about the way they perceive that environment. These words will reflect the three components that give a place its identity: its physical appearance, the human activities that take place there and the meanings that the buildings and activities have for people. They also tell us something about the attitudes and experiences of the people who live in, or visit, a place. This chapter introduces some fieldwork activities that explore the words that people use to describe places. Using these words can help students to find out more about the place, the people who go there and their perceptions of the local community and environment.

A simple starting point for this activity is for students to ask members of the public to offer words that describe a place. These words can then be processed into categories, either by using a spreadsheet (Figure 15) or by putting them onto cards. An alternative is to ask the students themselves to list descriptive words in the field. This has the benefit of encouraging students to examine their own perceptions of an environment. A further approach is to work as a large group with students calling out descriptive words and writing down some of those that have been suggested by other people. This allows each individual to hear the perceptions of others and provides support to those who are less able to think of interesting adjectives. A further simplification is to provide a word bank from which the students can ring the words that best describe their view of a place. While this limits the choice of words to some extent, the students could be encouraged to add their own words if they felt able to.

- Collate the words by typing them all into the first column of a spreadsheet
- In the next column type 'p' in the rows for each word that is positive and 'n' for those which are negative. A number of words may be neutral and these cells can be left blank
- Sort the words by the positive/negative column
- A further column could be added to show themes, such as 'environment', 'history' and 'people'. The words can be sorted again based on these themes.
- Use cut and paste to create a table of sorted responses

Figure 15: *Using a spreadsheet to work with descriptive words.*

Exemplar 1: Using descriptive words to compare social areas

Figure 16 shows words used by residents of Aberystwyth to describe the part of town in which they live. They were collected as part of an AS level study of social areas which also included a range of housing and environmental surveys. The table illustrates how this activity produces both quantitative and qualitative data, each making its own contribution to developing understanding of the town. The numerical data (percentages of negative words) can be plotted as located bars or proportional circles to provide a simple spatial comparison of perceptions of different areas. Analysis of the words themselves reveals more detail and variety about what the people who live in each area feel about their part of the town.

McKenzie and White (1982) argue that processing and discussing the meaning of information can help to develop conceptual learning. In this activity, this is achieved by the process of sorting words as well as by the analysis of the results. Sorting words into categories encourages discussion over the meanings intended by the people who said them. This is illustrated by the example in Figure 16, in which words such as 'multicultural' and 'student orientated' could be interpreted as positive or negative, depending on an individual's perception. Further discussion can take place when analysing the results. The percentages of positive and negative words in Figure 16 show that residents of central areas appear to experience more problems, often related to traffic, suggesting lower environmental quality in these parts of the town. While providing some answers, the words can also raise useful questions. For the words in Figure 16, these might include 'what makes an area "good for the young"? and 'why is the central district experiencing renovation?'.

Exemplar 2: Using descriptive words to compare perceptions of a place

The degree to which a person becomes attached to a place is strongly influenced by the amount of time that they have spent there. This creates differences in the levels of identification with a place between visitors ('outsiders') and locals ('insiders') (Pocock, 1983; Relph, 1976). Descriptive words can be used to compare these perceptions. When asking the respondents to offer descriptive words, the student should record whether the respondents are visitors or locals (their gender and an estimate of their age might also be helpful). This information can then be used as a basis for sorting the words.

Using descriptive words to develop literacy

The completed lists can be used as a resource to support a piece of writing. An example using the fieldwork illustrated in Figure 16 might be to take on the role of a resident and write a letter to a local newspaper about the problems of living in a certain part of town. The table can be used as a word bank from which adjectives used by people of the same age group can be taken. If the words have been sorted into different themes, these could

	Outer areas		Central areas	
Enumeration district	FC02	FC03	FC01	FF02
Descriptive words	**quiet**	**cosmopolitan**	**cultural centre**	**beautiful**
	Victorian	**quite good for**	**of Wales**	**pleasant**
	family orientated	**parking**	**community spirited**	**villagey**
	peaceful	**old church**	**friendly**	**pretty**
	cultural	**the best part**	**quiet**	**tranquil**
	very nice	**views**	**handy for shops**	**good community**
	Victorian	**rich area**	**quiet**	**spirit**
	buildings	**quiet**	**good access to town**	**pretty**
	retro chic	**nice houses**	**good community**	**good shopping**
	cultural	**peaceful**	**busy**	**things to do**
	rural	**pleasant**	**quiet**	old fashioned
	middle class	**quiet**	**compact**	congested
	quiet	**lovely views**	parking problems	traffic
	secluded	**good for the young**	small pavement	noisy
	affluent	**peaceful**	heavy traffic	not much space on
	beautiful	**pleasant**	busy roads	the narrow roads
Key	**pleasant**	**nice place to live**	quite congested	*a lot of renovation at*
positive	**friendly**	**crime free**	not very attractive	*the moment*
negative	nothing to do	**very little traffic**	unimpressive	
neutral	boring	**social**	dangerous	*busy*
	parking problems	**safe**	loud	
	hospital traffic	**well kept**	narrow	
	busy	busy road	*multicultural*	
	slow	nightmare in Summer	*student orientated*	
	steep	flat	*should have been*	
		lots of university students	*made a city*	
		ethnically diverse		
Total words	24	26	24	16
Negative words	5	2	10	5
% negative words	21%	8%	42%	31%

Figure 16: *Words used by local people to describe districts of Aberystwyth.*

be used to organise ideas into paragraphs. A further example could be to use the table of words as a resource for writing a letter to a friend describing why they have moved to a place and how they feel about living there. The words could also be used as the basis for a piece of writing or a presentation to the class about the problems that are experienced in the place that they have visited and what could be done to manage them.

| The green grass swaying |
| Distant foggy horizon |
| Jigsaw puzzle fields |

| Rocky and Peaceful |
| The candy-floss blue white sky |
| Dreamy atmosphere |

| Tall spiky mountains |
| Dim horizon, fading light |
| Plane high above us |

Figure 17:
Haiku poems written by three year 8 students at the Stiperstones, Shropshire.

An alternative to prose is to use the words as the basis for poetry. Job (1999) illustrates how the simplicity of Haiku poetry makes it appropriate to this form of fieldwork. A Haiku poem follows a strict structure with three lines of five, seven, then five syllables respectively (Figure 17). Working with words to fit them into this structure develops literacy skills and also enables students to develop the emotional side of their response to the place that they have visited (Slater, 1992).

Photo: © Helen Sail

Photos: © Helen Sail

Photo: © Helen Sail

6: Conclusion

It is hoped that reading this book will encourage teachers to reflect on the approaches to teaching and learning that they use in the field. Although quantitative methods are often favoured in schools, there is a great deal of variety in the type of activities that can be used. Which approach is chosen will be affected by the previous experience and preference of the teachers involved, but is likely to be most strongly influenced by the purpose of the trip. There is a high degree of freedom in the choice of methods when the purpose of a fieldwork exercise is to teach concepts and case studies for use in examinations, and of course there is even greater flexibility in key stage 3. However, if the students are undertaking coursework or preparing for a fieldwork-based examination, the focus is likely to be on the development of quantitative skills using the enquiry or field research approach. Bradford's (1995) assertion that the examination specifications tend to encourage the use of field research in GCSE and A level coursework remains true, even after the more recent revisions that have taken place. Teachers are understandably reluctant to put their students' examination prospects at risk by choosing an approach to fieldwork that is out of line with the expectations of their examination board.

There is, however, plenty of scope for using experiential fieldwork to support quantitative methods in GCSE and A level geography. Acclimatisation activities can be used at the start of a fieldwork exercise to get students thinking and increase awareness of what might be different and interesting about the place being studied. This provides them with a context for subsequent activities in an unfamiliar environment. If the fieldwork can then be tailored to answer the questions that arise from acclimatisation, this may well lead to greater ownership of the work and higher levels of motivation. Experiential methods can also be used to provide data that could be used in GCSE and A level coursework. Sound maps and descriptive words are two examples of qualitative activities that can add subtle shades of information to the more precise quantitative data.

However, perhaps the most important contribution that experiential fieldwork can make towards improving examination performance is by developing conceptual understanding, particularly in the light of the questions that have been raised over the suitability of quantitative techniques for this purpose. By encouraging heightened use of the senses and affective learning, experiential activities can help students to make a connection with the environment, to think more deeply and to remember what they have learned. Understanding will also be enhanced by the active participation of students in their learning in the field (MacKenzie and White, 1982).

The discussion in chapters 2 and 3 has shown that experiential fieldwork has a range of other purposes that can result in very different outcomes to the mainstream approaches. Perhaps the most fundamental of these is getting students to experience the place they are visiting, rather than just passing through. If they connect to an environment on an affective level, students may be encouraged to care more about what is happening there. It is this type of response that underlies the development of outcomes such as concern for nature, sense of place, aesthetic awareness and political literacy. Some of these goals might perhaps be viewed as ideals to aim for, rather than outcomes that can be expected of every student. Nevertheless, experiential methods can have an important part to play if the purpose of fieldwork is to educate the whole person as well as to prepare students for examinations and careers.

There do, however, remain concerns over experiential fieldwork that might discourage some teachers from using this approach. Job (1996) recognises how experiential methods can result in fairly superficial, descriptive outcomes. One way to address this is through effective questioning that challenges students to explain ideas and use higher order thinking skills. Taylor (2004) identifies how qualitative, subjective work can be difficult to assess, particularly when done in groups, as it may not correspond to existing assessment criteria and also because the students' responses may be hard to anticipate. She suggests using an approach taken from Leat and McGrane (2000) in which level descriptors are developed from samples of work that represent the range of performance. Taylor also shows how peer- and self-assessment using the creativity wheel (Durbin, 2003) can be a useful way for students to judge the value of subjective work and identify how improvements might be made.

It is also recognised that teachers may find it challenging to work with what are possibly unfamiliar methods. One way forward is to involve specialist drama, art or English teachers in planning and delivering fieldwork. This can be an effective way for geography teachers to pick up skills and techniques from these subject areas. Equally, as students become more familiar with experiential fieldwork they will gain in confidence and become used to practising skills from other subjects in geography.

Departments that are willing to make cross-curricular connections and embrace innovation will find that new ideas for fieldwork will emerge. Some ways forward might include:

- Creative use of a digital camera, perhaps with each student photographing the feature that they feel epitomises a place
- Using cartoons, for example by one student describing a scene to another, who draws it quickly without looking
- Developing questions to encourage thinking skills, illustrated in chapter 3, with further examples available in Job (1999, 2002)
- Encouraging empathy with others through the use of drama, illustrated in Biddulph and Bright (2003) and Caton (2001)
- Devising town trails to include a variety of experiential activities, the route perhaps being decided by the students. An example of how students might develop a town trail for users with special needs, devised by Dove (1997), is illustrated in Caton (2006)
- Reading poems about places and landscapes in the field (see Job, 1999). Students might use the styles and poetic devices in this published work to create their own poems that reflect their perceptions of a place or landscape.

In the past few years, a collection of fresh, creative ideas have invigorated geography teaching in the classroom. This book has aimed to show that there are also plenty of exciting fieldwork activities available. While many of these have been around for some years, it is only recently that they have started coming to the attention of more than a small minority of geography teachers. When reflecting on the purposes of their fieldwork programmes, geography departments may like to consider what experiential techniques have to offer. I hope this book has shown that using this approach will help students not just to understand, but also to think and care more about their world.

Bibliography

Biddulph, M. and Bright, G. (2003) *Dramatically Good Geography*. Sheffield: Geographical Association.

Black, P. and Wiliam, D. (1998) *Inside the Black Box: Raising standards through classroom assessment*. London: School of Education, Kings College.

Bradford, M. (1995) 'The new A level and AS geography syllabuses', *Teaching Geography*, 20, 3, pp. 145-8.

Brough, E. (1983) 'Geography Through Art' in Huckle, J. (ed) *Geography Education: Reflection and action*. Oxford: Oxford University Press.

Brownsword, R. (1998) 'Developing Empathy Through Language', *Teaching Geography*, 23, 1, pp. 16-21.

Butt, G. (2001) *Theory Into Practice: Extending writing skills*. Sheffield: Geographical Association.

Caton, D. (2001) 'An encounter with nature on Box Hill', *Teaching Geography*, 26, 3, pp. 139-41.

Caton, D. (2006) 'Real world learning through geographical fieldwork' in Balderstone, D. (ed) *Secondary Geography Handbook*. Sheffield: Geographical Association pp. 60-73.

Cosgrove, D. and Daniels, S. (1989) 'Fieldwork as theatre: a week's performance in Venice and its region', *Journal of Geography in Higher Education*, 13, 2, pp. 169-83.

Counsell, C. (1997) *Analytical and Discursive Writing at Key Stage Three*. London: Historical Association.

Daniels, S. (1992) 'Place and the geographical imagination' *Geography*, 77, 4, pp. 310-22.

Dove, J. (1997) 'Perceptual geography through urban trails', *Journal of Geography in Higher Education*, 21, 1, pp. 79-88.

Durbin C. (2003) 'Creativity – criticism and challenge in geography', *Teaching Geography*, 26, 2, pp. 64-9.

Fien, J. (1992) *Education For the Environment: Critical curriculum theorising and environmental education*. Geelong, AUS: Deakin University Press.

Foskett, N.H. and Kent, A. (2002) 'Fieldwork in the school geography curriculum: pedagogical issues and development' in Smith, M. (ed) *Teaching Geography in Secondary Schools*. London: Routledge Falmer, pp. 160-181.

Frew, J. (1993) *Advanced Geography Fieldwork*. Walton on Thames: Nelson Thornes.

George, D. (1997) *The Challenge of the Able Child*. London: David Fulton.

George, J., Clarke, J., Davies, P. and Durbin, C. (2002) 'Helping students to get better at geographical writing', *Teaching Geography*, 27, 4, pp. 156-59.

Goodey, B. (1982) 'Values in place: interpretations and implications from Bedford' in Gold, J. and Burgess, J. (eds) *Valued Environments*. London: Allen and Unwin, pp. 10-34.

Hall, D. (1981) 'Changing outlooks in geography' in Weigand, P. and Orrell, K. *New Leads in Geographical Education: Papers from the 1981 Leeds conference in geographical education.* Sheffield: Geographical Association.

Harvey, P.K. (1991) *The Role and Value of A Level Geography Fieldwork: A case study.* Unpublished PhD thesis, University of Durham.

Hawkins, G. (1987) 'From awareness to participation: new directions in the outdoor experience', *Geography*, 72, 1, pp. 217-22.

Holmes, D. and Farbrother, D. (2000) *A-Z Advancing Geography: Fieldwork.* Sheffield: Geographical Association.

Huckle, J. (1981) 'Humanistic geographical education – an introduction' in Weigand, P. and Orrell, K. *New Leads in Geographical Education: Papers from the 1981 Leeds conference in geographical education.* Sheffield: Geographical Association.

Job, D. (1996) 'Geography and environmental education: an exploration of perspectives and strategies' in Kent, A., Lambert, D., Naish, M. and Slater, F. (eds) *Geography in Education: Viewpoints on teaching and learning.* Cambridge: Cambridge University Press, pp. 22-49.

Job, D. (1999) *New Directions in Geographical Fieldwork.* Cambridge: Cambridge University Press/Queen Mary Westfield College.

Job, D. (2001) 'Fieldwork for a change', *Teaching Geography*, 26, 2, pp. 67-71.

Job, D. (2002) 'Towards deeper fieldwork' in Smith, M. (ed) *Aspects of Teaching Secondary Geography: Perspectives on practice.* London: RoutledgeFalmer/ Open University.

Job, D., Day, C. and Smyth, T. (1999) *Beyond the Bikesheds: Fresh approaches to fieldwork in the school locality.* Sheffield: Geographical Association.

Leat, D. and McGrane, J. (2000) 'Diagnostic and formative assessment of students' thinking', *Teaching Geography*, 25, 1, pp. 4-7.

Lenon, B.J. and Cleves, P.G. (1994) *Techniques and Fieldwork in Geography.* London: Collins Educational.

Ley, D. (1992) 'Qualitative methods: reshaping a tradition', *Journal of Geography in Higher Education*, 16, 2, pp. 167-70.

MacKenzie, A.A. and White, R.T. (1982) 'Fieldwork in geography and long term memory structure', *American Education Research Journal*, 19, 4, pp. 623-32.

McPartland, M. and Harvey, P. (1987) 'A question of fieldwork', *Teaching Geography*, 12, 4, pp. 162-64.

Palmer, J. and Neil, P. (1994) *The Handbook of Environmental Education.* London: Routledge.

Pocock, D. (1983) 'Geographical fieldwork: an experiential perspective', *Geography*, 68, 4, pp. 319-25.

Randall, D. (1999) *Teaching Green – A parent's guide to education for life on Earth.* London: Green Print, Merlin Press.

Reid, L.A. (1986) *Ways of Understanding and Education.* Oxford: Heinemann.

Relph, E. (1976) *Place and Placelessness*. London: Pion.

Rowles, G.D. (1978) 'Reflections on experiential fieldwork' in Ley, D. and Samuels, M.S. *Humanistic Geography: Prospects and problems*. London: Croom Helm, pp. 173-93.

Rynne, E. (1998) 'Utilitarian approaches to fieldwork', *Geography*, 83, 3, pp. 205-13.

Schafer, R.M. (1977) *The Tuning of the World*. New York, NY: Knopf.

Seamon, D. (1979) *A Geography of the Lifeworld*. London: Croom Helm.

Slater, F. (1992) 'Sea, Sand and Haikus: Linking geography with art and English', *Teaching Geography*, 17, 1, pp. 19-21.

Slater, F. (1994) 'Education through geography: knowledge, understanding, values and culture', *Geography*, 79, 2, pp. 147-63.

Smith, P. (1993) 'Arena: A place is a piece of environment that has been claimed by feelings', *Journal of Geography in Higher Education*, 17, 2, pp. 209-11.

Speake, J. and Fox, V. (2000) 'Investigating culturally-led urban regeneration', *Teaching Geography*, 25, 2, pp. 56-60.

Taylor, L. (2004) *Re-Presenting Geography*. Cambridge: Chris Kington Publishing.

Tuan, Y.F. (1974) *Topophilia*. London: Prentice Hall.

Van Matre, S. (1979) *Sunship Earth: An acclimatisation programme for outdoor learning*. Martinsville, IN: American Camping Association.

Ward, C. and Fyson, A. (1973) *Streetwork: The exploding school*. London: Routledge.

Wittrock, M.C. (1974) 'Learning as a generative process', *Educational Psychologist*, 11, pp. 87-95.

Wooldridge, S.W. and East, W.G. (1951) *The Spirit and Purpose of Geography*. London: Hutchinson.